Volume Three

HEADS

Volume Three

HEADS

Curtis J. Badger

STACKPOLE BOOKS

Published by
STACKPOLE BOOKS
Cameron and Kelker Streets
P.O. Box 1831
Harrisburg, PA 17105

Printed in the United States of America

10 9 8 7 6 5 4 3 2 1

First Edition

Cover design by Tracy Patterson with Caroline Miller

Interior design by Marcia Lee Dobbs

Cover photo: Redhead drake carved by Jett Brunet, photographed by Dan Williams. Reprinted with permission from *Wildfowl Carving and Collecting* magazine.

Library of Congress Cataloging-in-Publication Data

Badger, Curtis J.
    Bird carving basics.

    Contents: Vol. 1. Eyes — v. 2. Feet — v. 3. Heads — [etc.]
    1. Wood-carving. 2. Birds in art. I. Title.
TT199.7.B33   1990   731.4′62   90–9491
ISBN 0–8117-2339-9 (v. 3)

Contents

Acknowledgments

A series such as this would not be possible without the generous cooperation of artists like Jim Sprankle, Don Mason, Mark McNair, and Martin Gates. Not only did they let me peer over their shoulders with my camera as they worked, but later they took the time to review the resulting photographs and to explain each intricate step in the carving process. Thanks for your patience, guys.

In writing this series, I have yet to meet a carver who was reluctant to share his or her carving techniques. The reason, perhaps, is that wildfowl art is a sharing process. Art doesn't exist in a vacuum; even the most talented artists have learned from others, and all the carvers I've met have been more than willing to pass along their expertise to those who are just beginning.

Not only are Jim, Don, Mark, and Martin gifted artists, they are outstanding teachers as well. Jim and Mark teach in the Ward Foundation Summer Seminar series in Salisbury, Maryland, and they conduct workshops in their private studios. Don and Martin have given private instruction, and Martin has been asked to join the faculty of a folk art school in North Carolina. Teaching is one of the traditions of wildfowl art, and each of these four artists carries on that tradition in an exemplary manner.

Introduction

Not so long ago, bird carving was synonymous with decoy making. It was an American folk art, a craft that began with the hunter's need for functional decoys to lure birds to the gun. And although a few refinements were added over the years, bird carving remained rooted in the tradition of waterfowl hunting until the 1970s.

Today, wildfowl art is an ever-widening discipline. Although it is still rooted in the hunting tradition, contemporary bird carving has incorporated a variety of visual experiences, producing carvings ranging from the super-realistic to the abstract.

The exciting thing about the field is the degree of change that has taken place in the last twenty years, and, as a corollary, the changes that might be contemplated in the next two decades. A contemporary exhibition of bird carvings will include not only birds that clearly show their hunting-decoy lineage but also abstract forms of birds in natural wood intended not to portray a particular species but to capture something universal about all wildfowl.

Wildfowl art is healthy because it has been able to embrace this wide spectrum of techniques and styles. There is no right or wrong in wildfowl art, only different methods of making similar statements. The artists included in this book, for example, represent a broad range of styles. Each artist has his own particular background, motivation, and vision, and his work reflects this. In each case the work is unique, and although the subject is birds, each artist's work tells us as much about the artist himself as about the birds depicted.

In art, we tend to reflect what we know and what we have experienced. Jim Sprankle became involved in bird carving after careers as a pitcher for the Dodgers and the Redlegs, a banker, and a business executive. While hunting in the Chesapeake Bay, he came across decoys carved by Steve and Lem Ward of Crisfield, Maryland, and immediately decided to take up carving. Jim's realistic carvings reflect the beauty of the real world, but they also express much about himself and about his life. You don't get to be a major-league baseball pitcher by having sloppy technique. If your curveball hangs, you won't be around for long. And both banking and business are exacting pursuits that require attention to detail and mastery of the finer points. Jim's carvings are like this; they reflect not an overall style but the mastery of a thousand small tasks.

Of the other three carvers in this book, Don Mason is most like Jim. Don is a young carver who has quickly gained a solid reputation with wins at the Ward World Championship and other carving competitions. His birds, like Jim's, are highly detailed and realistic. Don is an electronics engineer with the National Aeronautics and Space Administration (NASA), a job that defines the word "exacting." Before he took up bird carving he raced dirt-track stock cars, an avocation that leaves little margin for error.

Mark McNair's carvings reflect a variety of passions: Northwest Indian folk art, music, history, the hunting tradition, and old-world craftsmanship. His carvings are visually the least complicated of the artists represented here, but they may be the most complex in terms of what goes into them. They reflect Mark's interests in design, in decoy history, and in carving and painting technique. The wood-duck head he carves in the exercise in this book is realistic, but it is carried off with a minimum of detail. Rather than scrupulously carving each feather, Mark suggests only a few details and lets the viewer provide the rest.

Martin Gates has only the skimpiest formal training in art, yet when he entered his first-ever carving competition he won first place in World Class Interpretive Sculpture at the Ward World Championships in 1987. He brings to the carving process a fascination with old-world craftsmanship and tools, a background in restoring European antiques, and an appreciation for the wading birds and raptors that live near his home in Gainesville, Florida. A distillation of all three of these elements has made Martin one of the most successful and unique young carvers of the 1980s. Martin began his career working in his dad's antique shop, restoring antique furniture imported from Europe. Often a complex figure or a piece of molding would be missing, and Martin would have to recreate the missing part using traditional tools and techniques. He quickly mastered the chisels and gouges, and since 1987 his carvings have won major awards and have been exhibited nationwide.

Success in art comes not so much from mastering techniques, although that is important, as from discovering a personal style, your own particular vision and method of expression. Whether it takes the form of highly detailed, realistic birds such as those by Jim Sprankle, or more impressionistic carvings like those of Martin Gates, is up to you.

This book is not so much a step-by-step instruction manual as a catalyst to help you discover your own particular vision and style. Art might begin with technique, but in order to grow it needs something that only you can bring to it, something that is yours and yours alone. So I hope that this series prompts you not only to discover something about the techniques of bird carving but to learn something about yourself as well.

1

Jim Sprankle
Carving a Cinnamon Teal Head

Jim Sprankle is a perfectionist, which is one of the reasons he's won dozens of awards as a professional wildfowl woodcarver. Another reason is that Jim is an artist, and he brings to the carving process not only technical virtuosity but a highly developed sculptural sense.

Jim's carvings are scrupulously realistic. An aviary is attached to his carving studio on Maryland's Eastern Shore, and Jim spends many hours studying and photographing birds before he begins a carving. These sessions help him not only to carve a bird with correct detail and scale but also to learn the nuances of avian behavior that give his carvings an edge in the competitions.

Jim uses as much reference material as he can muster. In addition to his aviary, he keeps a comprehensive file on every species of bird he carves. This reference material might include photographs, books, study skins, taxidermy specimens, and videotapes. He also uses plastic casts of heads and bills that show every bump and wrinkle. With such material, Jim is able to produce birds that are remarkably lifelike.

In this session he carves and textures the head of a cinnamon teal. (In volume one of this series Jim inserts the eyes in this cinnamon teal head, and in volume four he carves and details the bill.) He uses a variety of grinders, cutters, stones, and burning tools in this session, beginning with a large carbide cutter to shape the cheek contour. As he begins this demonstration, the head has already been roughed out and the bill carved and detailed; the eyes have been located and the sockets drilled.

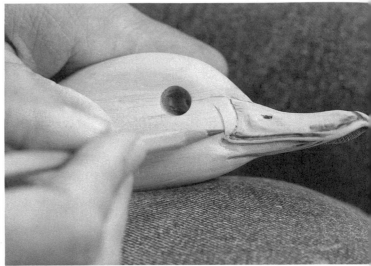

Jim begins carving the head by shaping the jowl area. He starts by drawing a small contour line behind the bill with a pencil, using a cast study bill as reference.

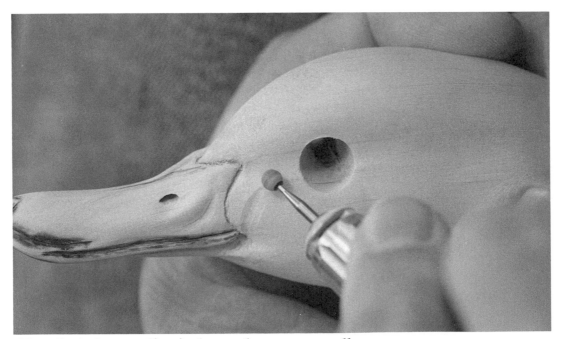

After the reference line is drawn, he uses a small diamond ball in a high-speed grinder to relieve the wood. "This curve is not always seen," says Jim. "On a gadwall drake it's very prominent, but not always on a cinnamon. But I like to add these little lumps and bumps. They give it a little more realism."

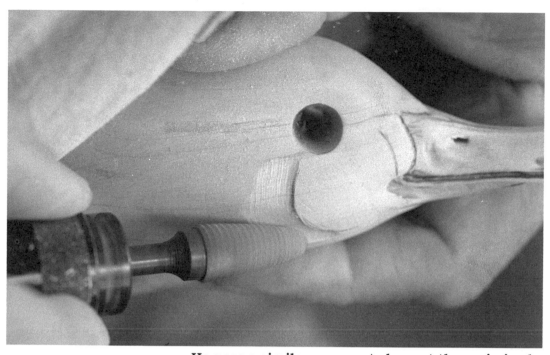

He uses a similar process to lay out the main jowl area. A contour line is drawn beginning below and slightly to the rear of the eye, then the area is relieved with a carbide cutter.

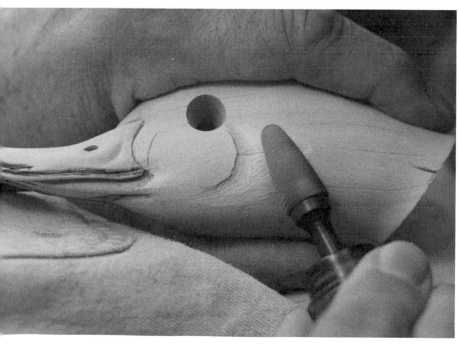

When the jowl has been relieved, Jim uses the carbide cutter to feather the area, creating a gentle swell rather than a sharply defined area.

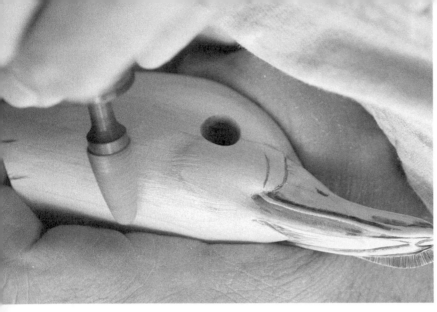

He uses the carbide tip
to blend the jowl area
with the curvature
of the neck. He follows
the same procedure on
both sides of the head.

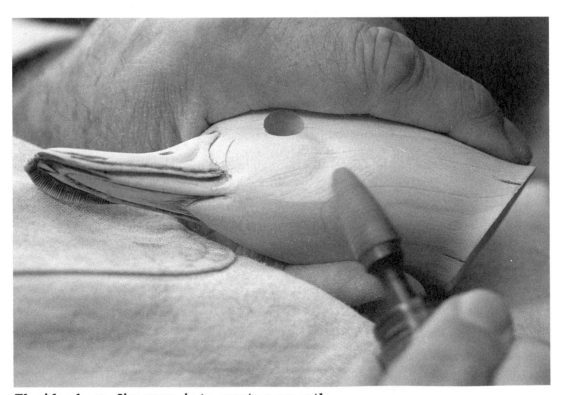

The idea here, Jim says, is to create a smooth
transition from the bill area to the jowl to the
neck. The large carbide cutter is a good tool for
these featherlike contour lines.

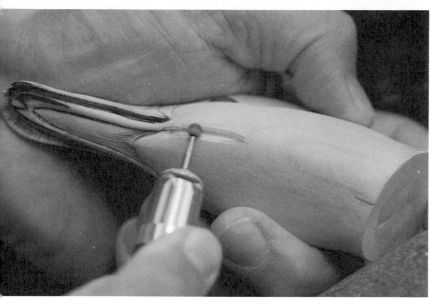

When the jowl area is complete, Jim uses his high-speed grinder with a round diamond cutter to shape the small indentation behind the lower mandible. "Again, we're adding some lumps and bumps," he says, "creating some realism."

With the "lumps and bumps" relieved and feathered, Jim is ready to texture the head. "It's imperative, before you put any texture on the head, to take a pencil and draw in the feather flow lines," he says. These lines act as a guide for feather flow. Be sure you're satisfied with the lines and flow at this stage. Pencil marks can be easily erased; carved details cannot.

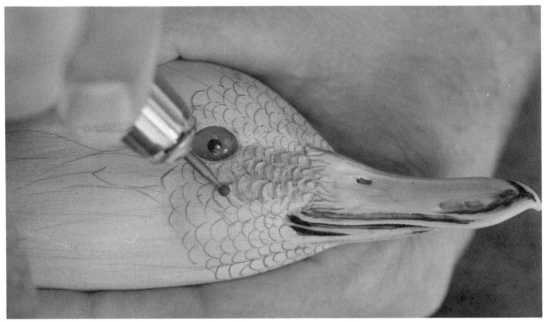

With the flow lines in place, Jim then uses a pencil
to draw each individual feather along the front of
the head, from the rear of the bill to just behind
the eyes. Then the high-speed grinder is used with
the smallest ceramic stone available to outline
each of those feathers.

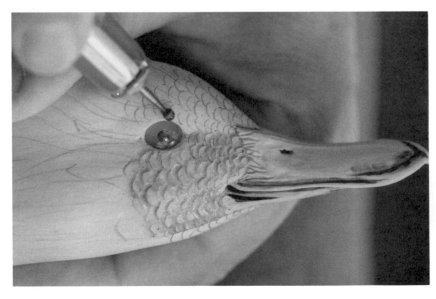

The technique
is used on
both sides of
the head,
and on the top
of the head.

After outlining each feather with the ceramic stone, Jim uses the pencil to redefine each feather line. These lines serve as a guide during the next step: detailing each feather with the burning pen.

The sharp tip of the burning pen is used to create individual barbs in each feather, a technique that will contribute greatly to the realism of the finished bird. The tip should be just hot enough to burn a groove into the wood. Jim explains, ''The cooler the tip, the more lines you can burn per inch.''

In this close-up, the individual feathers and barbs are shown. Note also the withered, slightly wrinkled, area at the rear of the bill. These lines were created with a number 9 lead pencil, and also add to the illusion of realism.

When the individual feathers are relieved, Jim reestablishes the feather flow with a pencil. The goal now is to create a smooth transition from the highly detailed burned area to the back of the head and the neck.

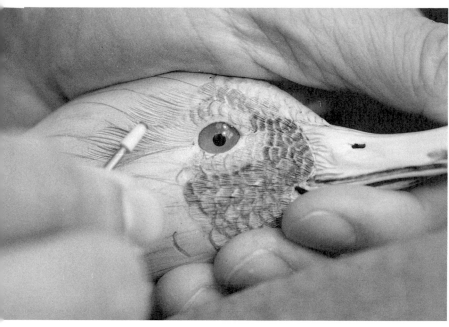

He begins just be-hind and above the eyeline with a ceramic stone. Here the feathers are longer and more sweeping, and the movement follows the flow of the pencil guidelines.

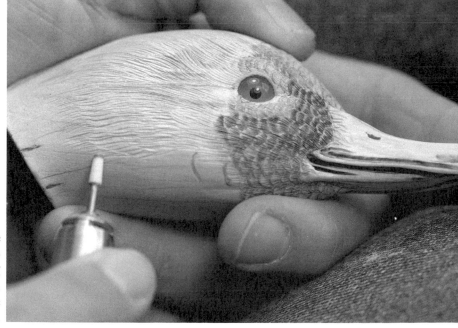

Jim uses the same ceramic stone to create the flowing lines below the eye, still following the pencil lines.

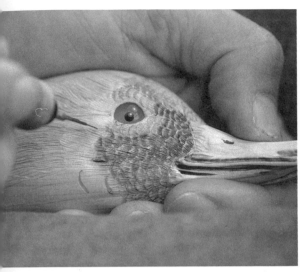

The lines simply feather the two areas together, eliminating the abrupt border. Only a few lines are necessary; Jim wants enough to create a visual flow between the two areas, but no more. When these lines are burned, the head is ready for final finishing and painting.

With both feather areas relieved by the stone or the burning pen, Jim uses the pen to create a smooth transition between the two areas. He does this by burning in longer, flowing lines that begin at the detailed feathers and extend rearward.

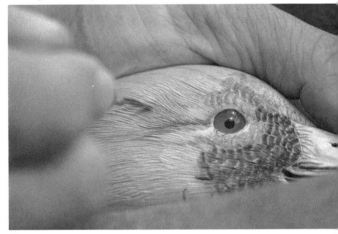

Jim's finished cinnamon teal hen.

2

Don Mason
Carving the Head of a Pintail

Until 1982 Don Mason spent most of his spare time driving dirt-track stock cars. When he wasn't driving them he was tinkering with them, attempting to squeeze extra horsepower from a souped-up Chevy.

In 1982 Don quit the racing circuit—too expensive, he says—and began looking for another avocation. That October he happened by the Ward Foundation Wildfowl Art Exhibition in Salisbury, Maryland, on his way to a race in Dover, Delaware, and he immediately became hooked on bird carving.

It's an unusual transition from stock-car racing to bird carving, but that's the way it happened for Don. "I bought a copy of Bruce Burk's book *[Game Bird Carving]* that day at the Ward Show, and I went home and carved a bufflehead," he says.

Since then, Don has converted his basement into a carving studio, and the only remnants of his racing career are a few snapshots tacked to his studio wall. His home, which overlooks the seaside marshes of Virginia's Eastern Shore, is filled with his carvings and ribbons won at a variety of carving competitions.

Don, who works in electronics at NASA, took a workshop with Pat Godin in Salisbury in 1985, and has worked diligently at developing his technique. For the past two years he has competed in open (professional) class and has chalked up wins at the Ward World Championship in Ocean City, Maryland, at the Mid-Atlantic in Virginia Beach, and at shows in Richmond, Virginia, Chestertown, Maryland, and Tuckerton, New Jersey.

Don specializes in realistic birds and uses a wide variety of reference material, including cast study parts, photographs, and videotapes. In this session, Don carves a pintail drake head. The bird is being carved with an open bill, and this will affect the shape of the head where it joins the bill. Don makes a series of wrinkles on the head at the base of the bill.

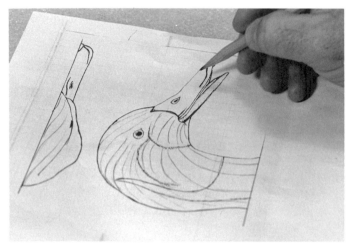

Don begins the pintail head and bill by drawing a pattern, using as reference color slides and a cast study bill. He draws both the side and top views and adds as much detail as possible, including position of eyes and nostrils, the nail on the bill, and the flow lines of feathers.

Once the pattern is drawn, he cuts it out and transfers the detail to wood. When he traces the side pattern, he marks the eye location because he will use a drill press to pre-drill the eye sockets before carving the head and bill.

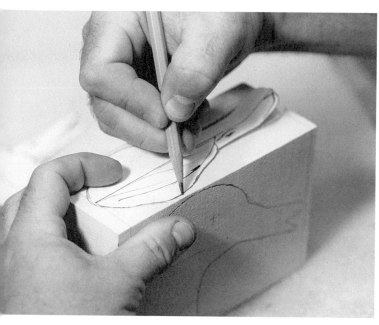

The top pattern is drawn
and the bill detail and feather
flow lines are transferred
to the wood.

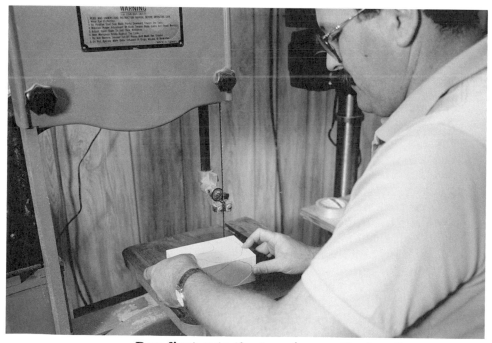

Don first cuts the top view on the bandsaw,
then the side view. This method gives him more
accuracy in placement and detail.

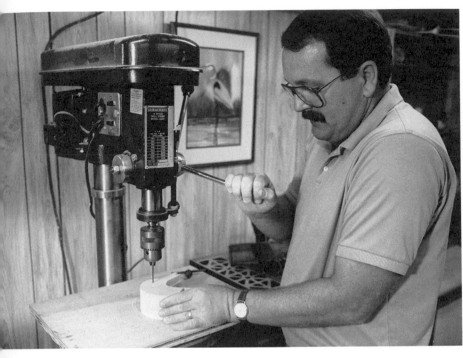

Don uses reference photos and study bills to determine exact eye placement on his pattern. He then transfers this location to the wood and uses the drill press to drill a pilot hole for the sockets. This method insures that the eye sockets will be aligned perfectly.

Don draws a center line around the head, neck, and bill of the bird. This line will serve as a high-point reference when rounding contours, and it will remain on the carving until it is ready for sanding. This line is essential for achieving the correct contour and for retaining the proper shape of the head.

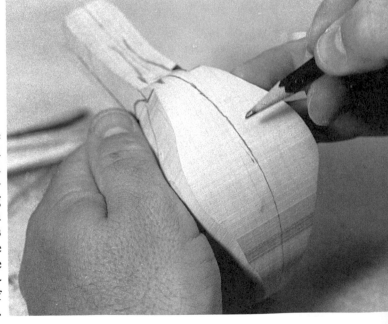

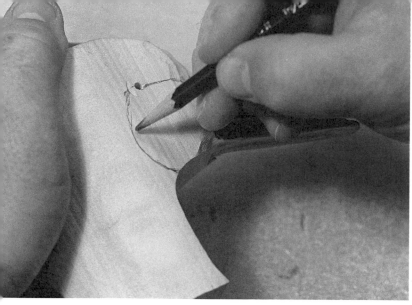

Don completes the bill of the carving first (his techniques are detailed in volume four of this series), then begins the head. He uses his reference drawing and the study head to sketch the eye channel and cheek line.

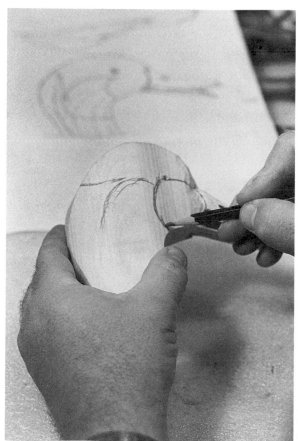

The lines indicate the positions of initial cuts that will begin the contouring and shaping process. Because Don began with a detailed and accurate head pattern, he uses it as a reference throughout the carving process.

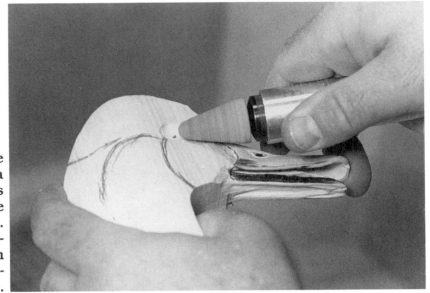

A large carbide cutter on a Foredom tool is used to cut the eye channel. Don begins cutting at a depth of about one-eighth inch.

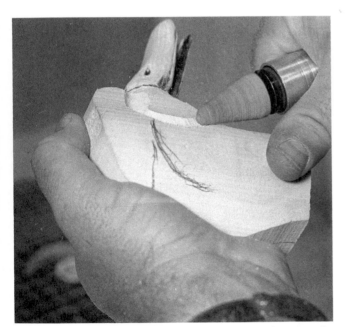

The eye channel extends through the eye position and downward to create a cheek area.

Don uses dial calipers to measure on his pattern the width of the head at the eye channel. This could also be measured using a cast study bill that includes head detail.

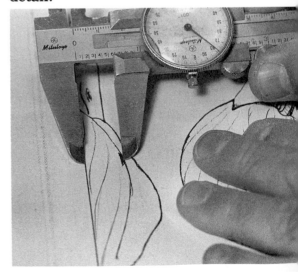

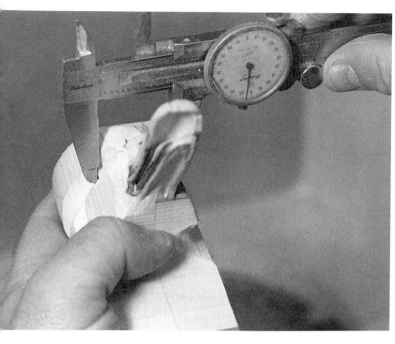

The measurement is then transferred to the work-piece. Don begins by removing small amounts of wood, gradually increasing the depth until the width of the head is correct.

Don does his heavy cutting and grinding in a vacuum box he made himself. The box uses a pair of fans and a series of filters to remove airborne particles.

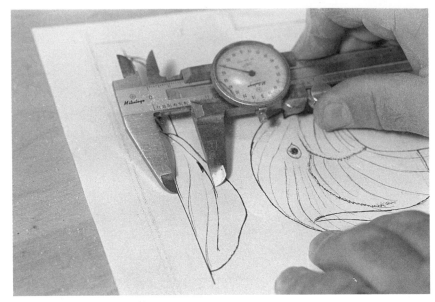

He now measures the width of the crown of the head at the widest point.

These lines, reaching from the upper ridge of the bill to the back of the head, define the crown of the head, and Don uses them as guides in shaping the head with a grinder.

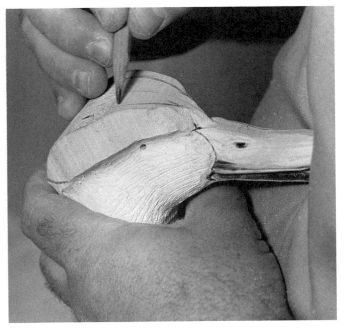

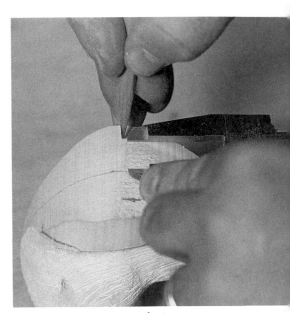

This measurement is transferred to the workpiece, and reference lines are drawn.

18

The carbide tip on the Foredom is used to round the top of the head, using the lines drawn previously as guides.

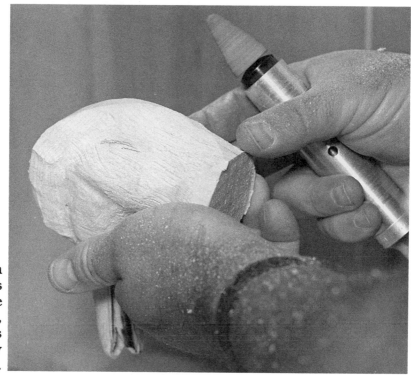

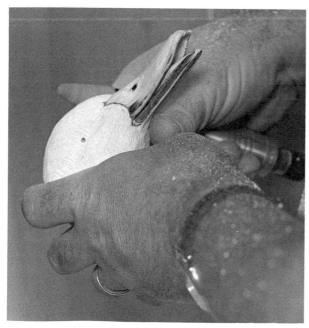

This large carbide tip is used to round off all the straight lines along the head. But it's important to leave the center line, which indicates the high point of the contour.

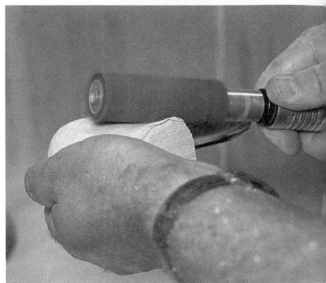

A small drum sander is used on the Foredom to round off edges and to remove marks left by the carbide tip. Don uses this drum to sand the larger areas of the head.

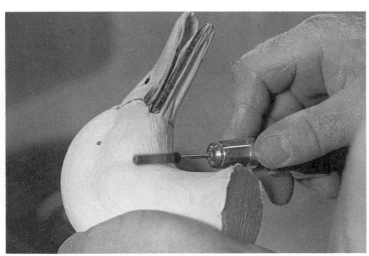

A small split mandrel with a piece of 120-grit paper is used to sand the less accessible areas.

The head is now finished, and Don is ready to add feather detail.

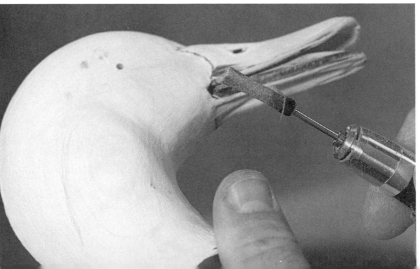

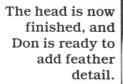

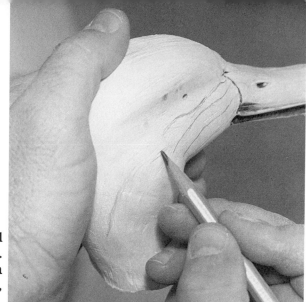

He begins by using a pencil to sketch the feather flow lines. These lines can be taken from a study bird, a photograph, or a pattern.

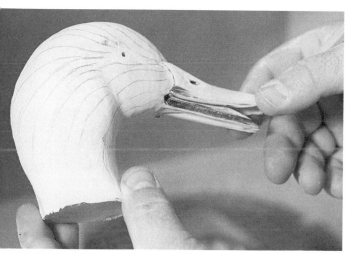

Note how the feather lines flow across and down the head. These lines will serve as guides when Don uses a stone to add texture lines.

Before he begins using the grinding stone, he sharpens it on an old diamond cutter, which flattens the tip of the grinding stone.

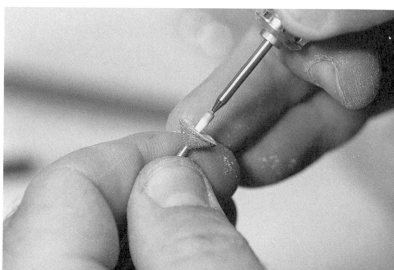

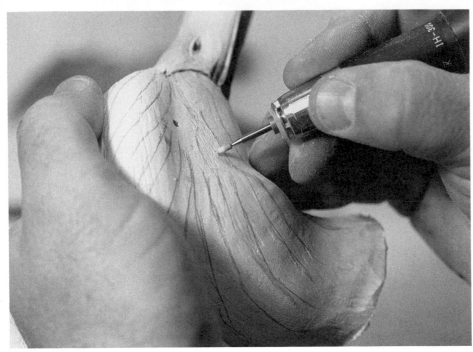

Don begins texturing at the front of the head, adding one small feather at a time with very short strokes of the stone.

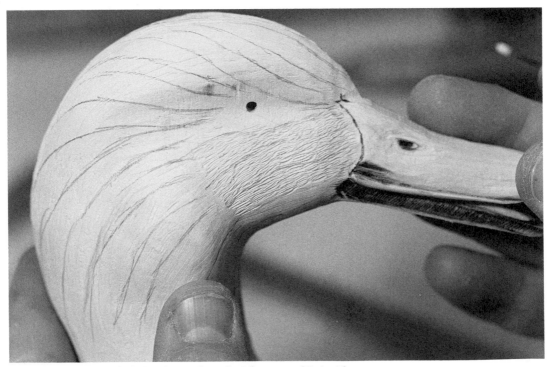

The stoning is finished on the cheek area. Note the direction and size of the texturing.

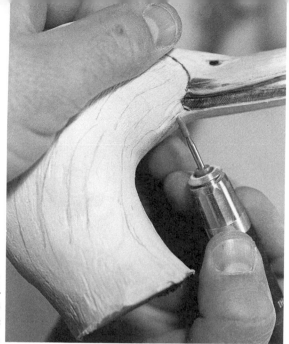

When a duck opens its bill, small wrinkles appear just behind the lower mandible where it is hinged to the jaw. Don uses the stone to add texture to this area.

A slightly coarser stone is used to texture the feathers behind the cheek area. These feathers are larger and fluffier, so the texturing technique should be bolder, with slightly deeper and longer cuts.

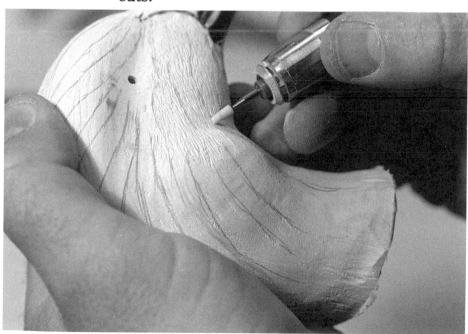

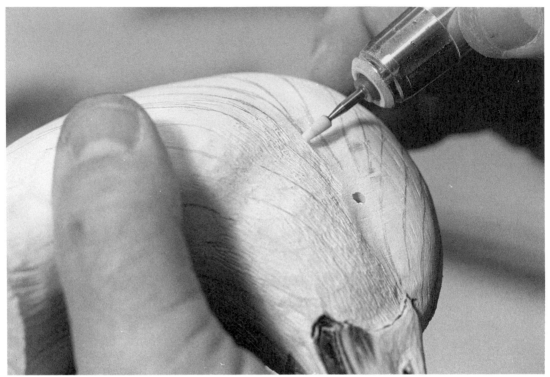

Here Don stones the feathers behind the eye
socket and along the side of the head.

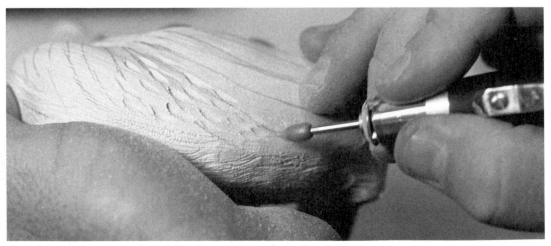

On the back of the head Don uses a pointed ruby
carver to create channels that will later resemble
fluffed feathers.

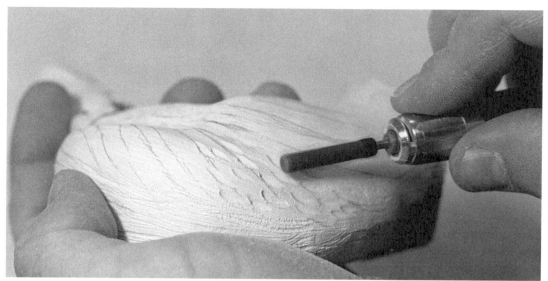

The grooves left by the ruby cutter are softened and rounded by using sandpaper on the split mandrel.

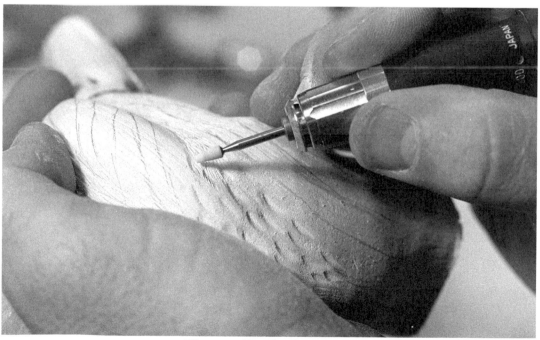

The small grinding stone cuts fine barbs over the grooves to establish a feather pattern.

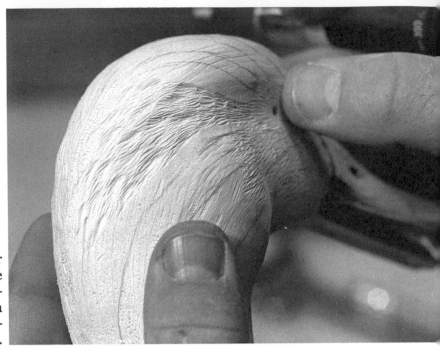

In this photo it is clear that the back of the head will have a fluffier appearance, with the illusion of overlapping feather groups.

The pintail head is now textured. At this point Don adds the eyes and eyelids.

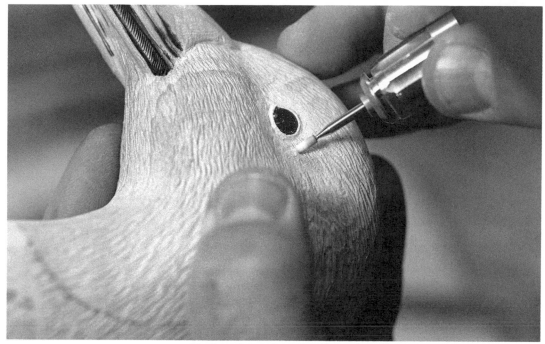

Before burning feather detail, Don uses a stoning tool to clean and reshape the texture covered by excess filler around the eye.

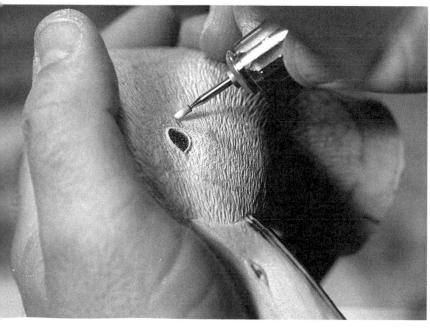

With texturing almost finished, Don goes over the head closely to ensure that the feather detail is complete.

The pintail head is now ready for burning.

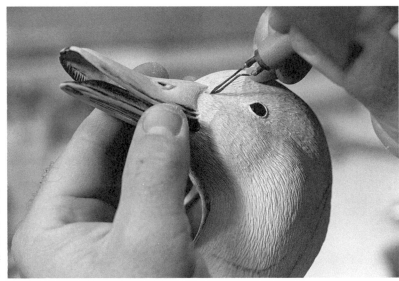

Don uses a fine burning tip on a low heat setting to burn the small feathers on the front of the head.

Feather detail is very intricate in this area, and the strokes with the burning tool should be short and fine.

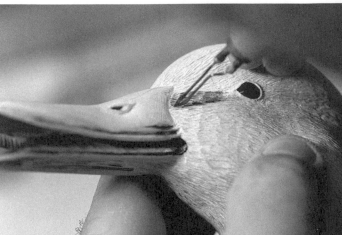

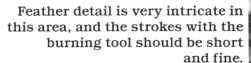

Burning strokes on the back of the head are longer and slightly more coarse than those immediately behind the bill.

The pintail head with burning completed.

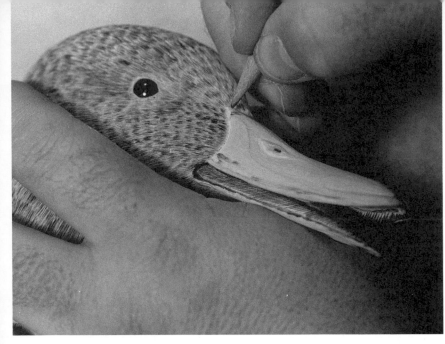

Only a few small details need to be added before the head is completed. A duck has slight wrinkles at the base of the bill, so Don uses a hard lead pencil to press wrinkles into the wood.

Pencil marks show wrinkles in the bill where it meets the head. The pencil leaves a slight indentation that will have the proper texture when painted.

30

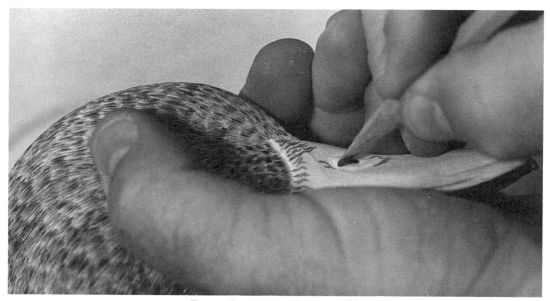

Don also uses the pencil to add small wrinkles around the nostrils.

Wrinkles should also be added along the nail on the upper mandible.

The finished head is trial-mounted on the roughed out pintail body.

The finished pintail drake.

3

Mark McNair
Carving a Wood-Duck Head

Mark McNair grew up in Connecticut and moved to the Virginia coast some twelve years ago. It is ironic that Mark's move to Virginia was very similar to that of one of his predecessors in wildfowl art, a Massachusetts shipbuilder named Nathan Cobb.

Cobb moved from New England to Virginia in the 1830s, almost 150 years before McNair did. Cobb settled in a little town called Oyster and later purchased a coastal island where he carved decoys and ran a sportsman's hotel. Mark has no plans for a hotel, but he came to Virginia at about the same age Cobb did, and, like Cobb, Mark spends his days making incomparable decoys in the hunting tradition. Mark lives on a farm overlooking Currituck Creek, some thirty miles northwest of where Nathan Cobb eventually settled.

Mark admires Cobb's craftsmanship, the "strong, sure hand" that enabled him to capture the essence of a bird with a minimum of detail. You see a lot of this in Mark's work; a minimalist practice of using the smallest gesture to capture something universal about a bird. But there's more. Mark is influenced by Northwest Indian art, by music, by history, by all the visual arts. His carvings are clean, graceful, and uncluttered, but they come from something more complex than they seem to. Mark's carvings are a melting pot of visual experience.

In this session, as he carves a wood-duck head, he attempts to keep the knifework to a minimum, adding only enough relief to suggest detail. Detail doesn't have to be deeply cut and dramatic to work, he says. A figure etched onto the face of a coin shows a great deal of detail, but it's all done within the space of a few one-thousandths of an inch.

Mark begins the carving process with a series of sketches that will serve as the mental "blueprints" for the carving. "All carvings begin as a concept," he says. "The idea has to come from somewhere. It doesn't come from a vacuum. It comes from a photograph, a carving, a painting, a live bird—perhaps an assimilation of all these things.

When I have an idea, I need to get the idea out of my head, so I draw first."

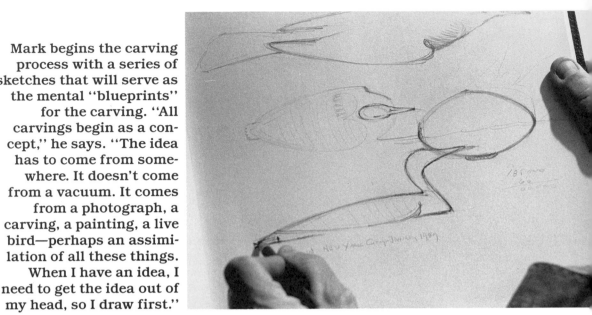

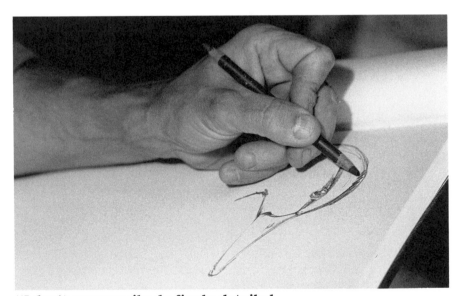

"I don't necessarily do finely detailed drawings, but I like to get the work out in front of me and think it through," says Mark. He does top, side, and front dimensions of a head. "The trick is to meld them into something that becomes more fourth dimensional, something that works visually from all angles."

In the preliminary work, the pencil is Mark's most important tool. "You can cross things out, you can draw things over, you can write three pages of notes. The pencil also has an eraser, so if you have a problem you can wipe it out. I don't do the sketches for anyone but myself. It's the first step in getting the idea out of my mind and into this world."

Once Mark sketches a profile he likes, he makes a wooden pattern and labels it. Here he sketches the side pattern of a wood-duck head onto a block of white cedar.

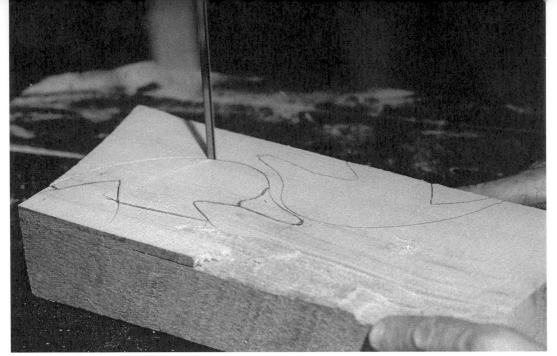

The profile is cut out on a bandsaw. The top
dimension will be cut later. The cedar is about two
inches thick, slightly thicker than the width of
the finished head.

The head should be cut so the grain of the wood
runs lengthwise with the head and along a vertical
bias, providing strength to thin areas such as the
bill.

Mark carefully uses the bandsaw to rough out the top profile of the head, removing about one-eighth inch of wood on each side. The thin pieces of wood removed at this stage make good patterns for future carvings.

Mark sketches the top view, "the second profile," on top of the head and bill. "I've already done this on paper, so I'm not doing it for the first time," he says. "The sketch is like a road map, it helps you plan where you're going. Unless you become comfortable with drawing, you're going to have a rough time carving. I draw a center line, and everything else is drawn off that line."

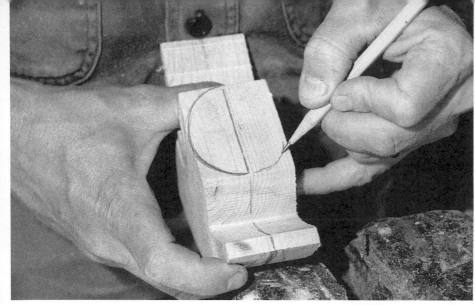

Mark roughs out the head wider than he will ultimately need. Here he marks the finished size of the neck so he won't cut away too much wood at the base of the neck.

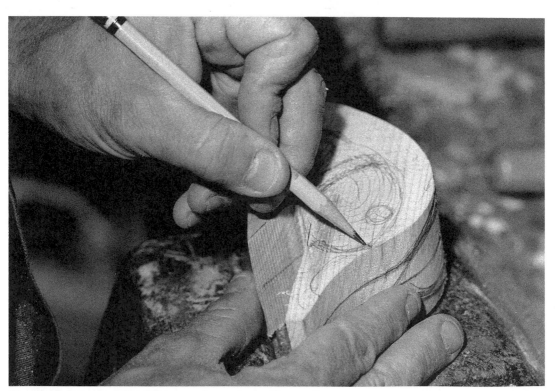

He sketches eye position and contour lines along the cheek of the bird, not as definite references, but simply to get a feel for what the bird will look like. "I like to use the pencil to create the illusion of depth, just to see how the head will develop."

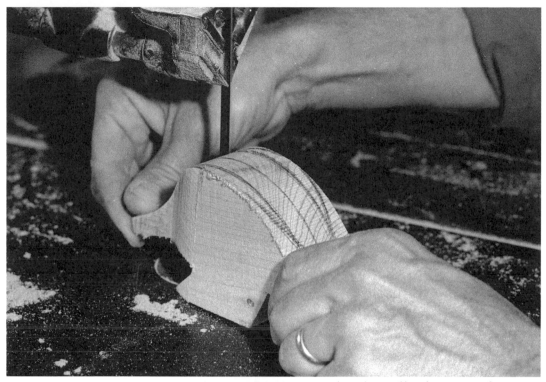

Here Mark cuts out what he calls the second profile, after sketching in the dimensions developed on his sketch pad.

Once the head is roughed out on the bandsaw, Mark uses a hatchet to remove excess wood. "It looks a bit coarse," he says, "but I don't carve the whole head with it and I don't do it this way to be old-fashioned. To me, it's a comfortable and efficient way to remove wood."

The hatchet must be kept sharp, as must all other tools. Mark uses the hatchet only to rough out the head. He believes in using the largest tool practical for doing a job.

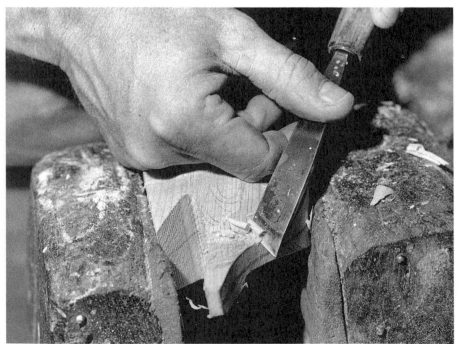

A skew chisel is used to further rough out the carving. Here Mark removes wood from the area where the bill meets the head.

Wood works better when cut askew, hence the design of the skew chisel.

Not much fine work will be done with the skew chisel, but it is used as an intermediate step, providing more precision than the hatchet.

A knife is used to further relieve the carving. Mark uses various knife-edged tools, depending on the job to be done. His knife, hatchet, and spokeshave all have blades roughly the same length; in choosing a tool Mark considers not only the correct blade but also the proper handle, which makes the blade usable for a particular task.

Once the head is roughed out with the bandsaw and hatchet, Mark alternates between the skew chisel and knife to carve contours.

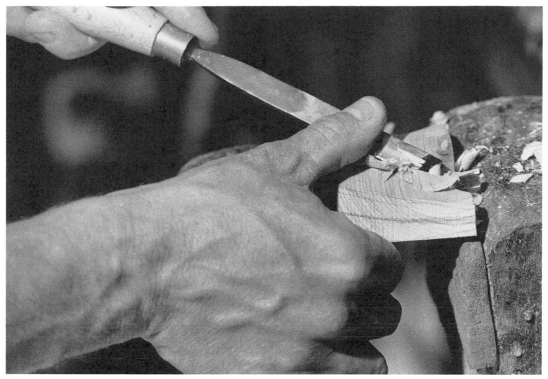

The center line, seen here along the back of the head, represents the high point of the head profile and will remain visible during most of the carving process.

With the carving roughed out, Mark uses a cabinet rasp to smooth the surface and create subtle contours. "The chisel and hatchet remove great chunks of wood," he says, "but the rasp gives a nice flowing look."

The half-round rasp is used under the neck to develop a graceful interior curve.

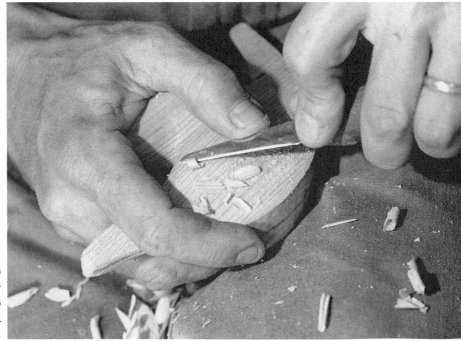

When Mark makes small adjustments he needs the precision of a knife.

He roughly sketches the eye and bill, then uses a fine rasp to smooth the cheek contour.

Beveling with the spokeshave creates a dramatic transition between the brow and the crest. "I like the spokeshave and use it a lot, but more frequently on bodies," he says. "The head has so many contours and they change so rapidly, the rasp is usually more appropriate. But for this step with the wood duck, it's a good tool."

He begins by using the knife to make a shallow cut along the pencil line separating the bill and head. "I carve the bill and head together because it helps me keep a pleasing line down the head and through the bill. The bill shouldn't look plugged into the head, it should be part of the head, it grows out of the head. That's why I wait until this point to separate the head and bill."

Now Mark is ready to carve eye and bill detail. "I've done all the detail so far with the pencil, and the form of the head is complete, so I'm not going to take off much wood. I'm not going to change the shape of the surface, just add some relief to it. You don't need to remove a lot of wood to create detail."

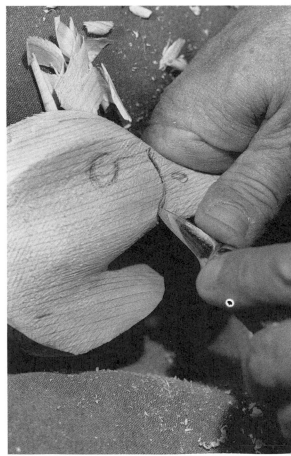

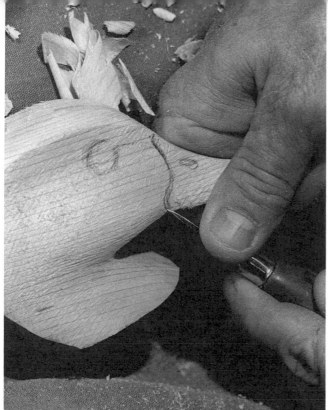

For the upper mandible, Mark cuts at a slight angle toward the back of the head. For the lower mandible, he angles the knife slightly forward. He emphasizes that the detail should be subtle and the cuts shallow. "You don't need to do anything dramatic, especially in areas like this where the separation is going to be painted. You don't have to emphasize the obvious."

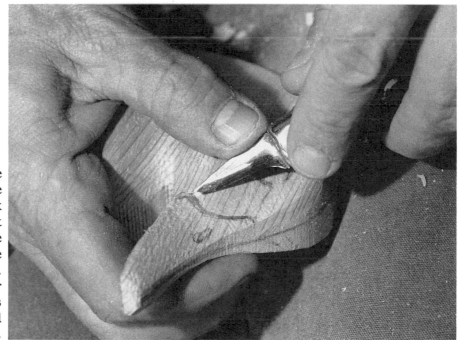

After the cuts are made along the bill line, Mark uses a knife to cut back to the line to distinguish the upper mandible. For the upper mandible, he cuts from the head toward the bill.

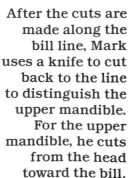

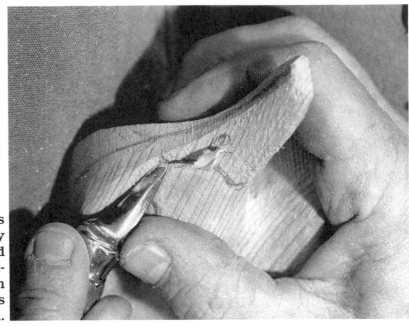

This cut is made at a very sharp angle, and the depth is shallow. Only a thin shaving of wood is removed.

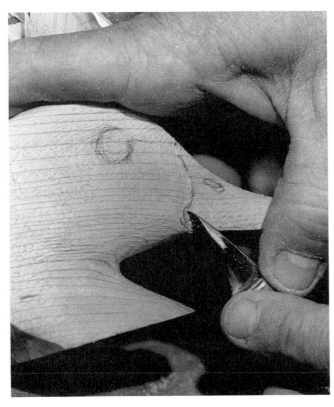

On the lower mandible, Mark cuts from the bill toward the head, again making a very shallow cut.

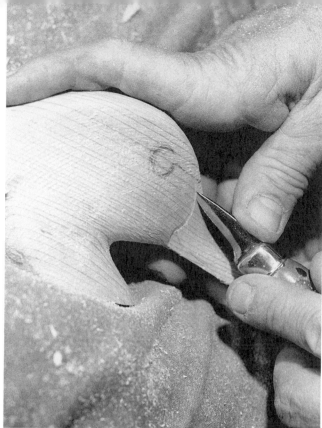

In this photo the bill is relieved, and Mark uses the knife to remove wood chips from the line. The same procedure is used on the other side of the bill.

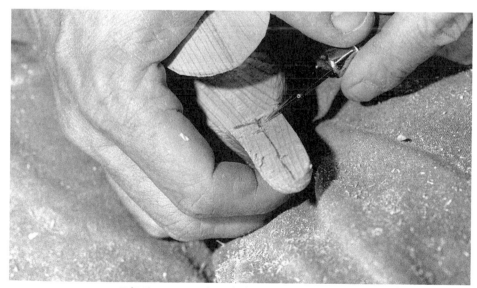

Little or no detail is carved on the bottom of the bill. Mark etches a wide V where the bottom of the bill meets the head. The center line is just a pencil mark made for reference.

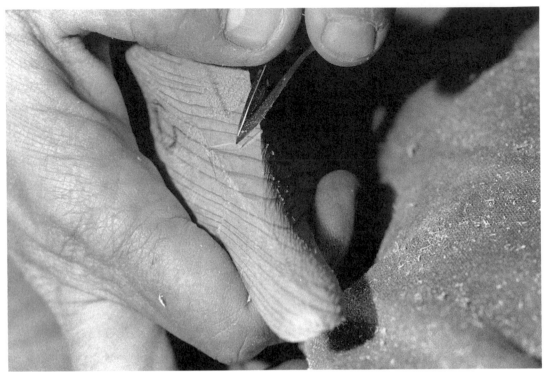

Mark carves a slight notch where the top of the bill meets the head to provide separation. Further separation will come during the painting process, so only shallow relief is needed here.

He uses a pencil to sketch the separation between the upper and lower mandibles.

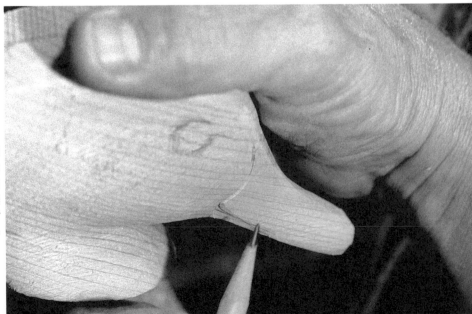

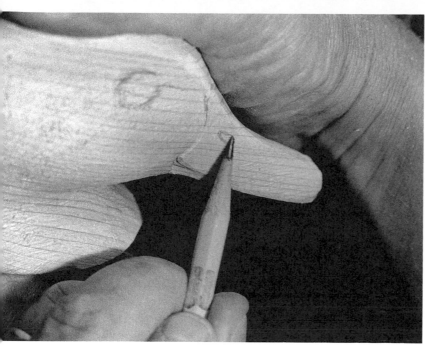

The nostril is also sketched at this time. Mark doesn't use study bills or reference photos. If the sketch doesn't look quite right, he'll erase it and redraw.

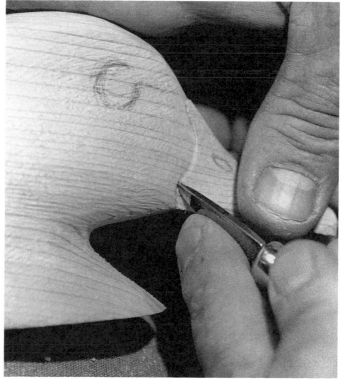

Mark begins the cut separating the mandibles along the base of the upper mandible and scribes a curve that flows into the pencil line he just drew. "To make this cut nice and clean, stick the knife in and pull it down in a slight arc. Instead of making it a straight linear cut, give it a little bit of flare."

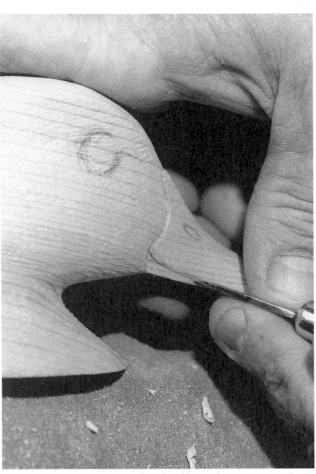

The cut is shallow, just enough to create visible separation between the mandibles. "All you're trying to do is to relieve the surface, to throw a shadow," he says.

After the initial cut is made, Mark undercuts it from below and removes a small sliver of wood.

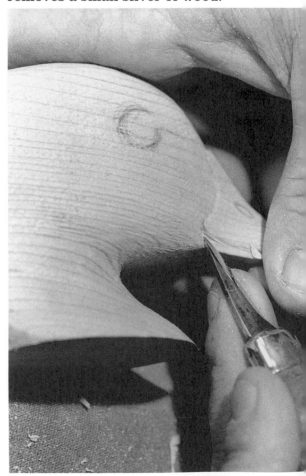

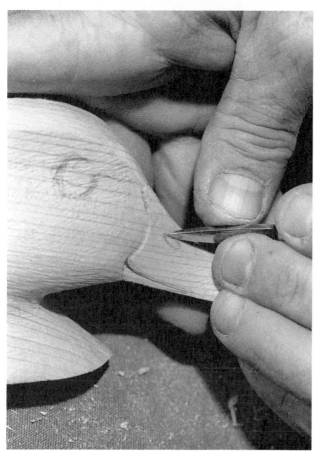

The nostril is carved with two cuts.
Mark first makes a shallow cut along the
top of the nostril.

Then an angled cut is made
from below, and the small
piece of wood is removed.

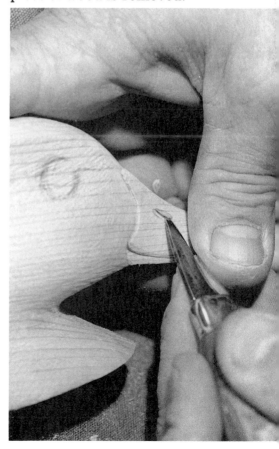

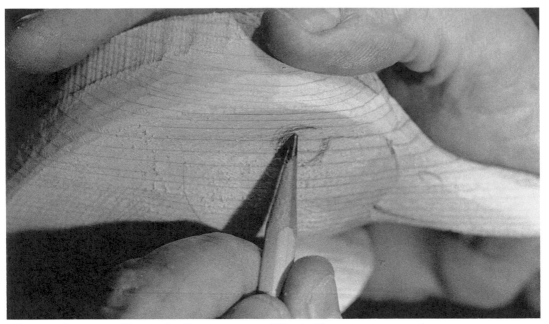

The eye is carved in a similar manner. First, the eye position is determined with the pencil. Mark will carve the eye in this bird instead of using a glass eye.

He begins by using the knife to carve a circle around the eye. If he were going to insert a glass eye, he would make the cut deeper to accommodate the eye and filler. The carved eye will be created with a minimum of detail.

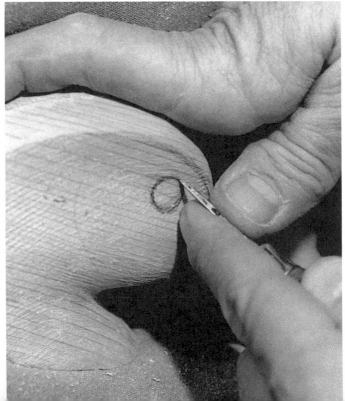

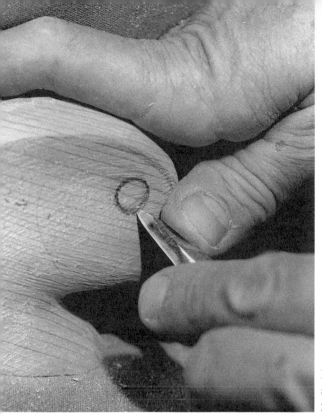

Mark uses the pencil line as a guide, scribing a circle around the circumference of the eye.

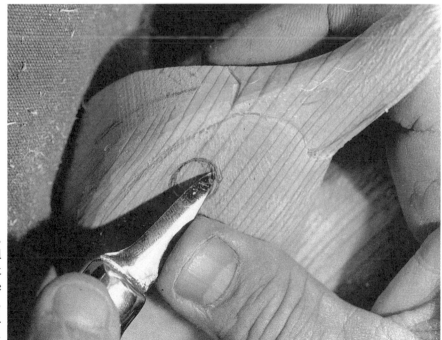

After the line is cut, the blade is used at an angle to cut back toward the line from the inside, creating the illusion of a convex eye.

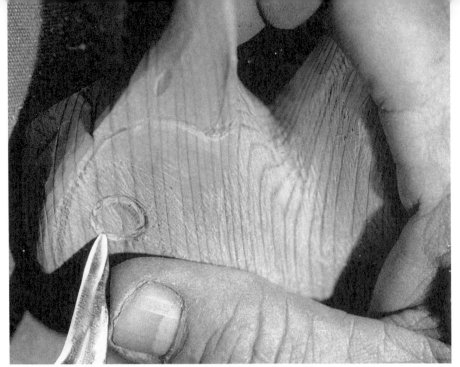

The knife is used to clean up the line after the cut
is made.

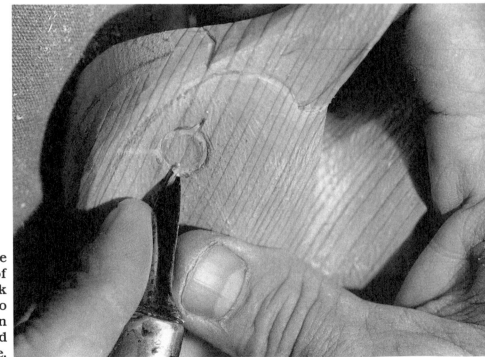

To create the
illusion of
an eyelid, Mark
carves two
small lines in
front of and
behind the eye.

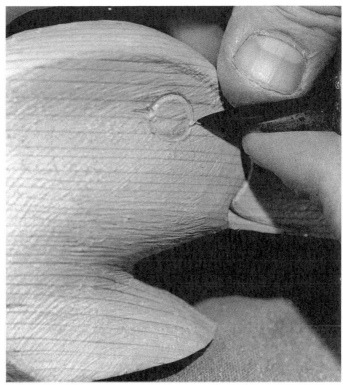

These lines create the illusion of eyelids, which are pink on the wood duck and are very prominent. The detail is small, but it is important in capturing the look of the species.

The bow sander is used to finish the head. The sander is made of a simple wooden frame with a strip of sandpaper stretched across the opening.

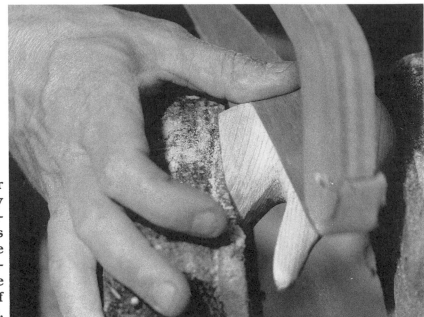

The bow sander is especially good at smoothing contours because the sandpaper conforms to the shape of the workpiece.

The finished wood-duck head is ready to be mounted on a body. Note the amount of detail that can be provided with just a few shallow lines.

4 Martin Gates

Carving the Head of an Eagle

Until 1987, Martin Gates had never carved a bird for competition. He had worked in his father's antique shop near Gainesville, Florida, restoring European antiques, and he had taken up carving part time after spending two months as an apprentice to Dan DeMendoza, a Florida artist who specializes in miniatures.

But in 1987 a fellow employee at the antique shop who happened to be a carver and member of the Ward Foundation talked Martin into entering the Ward World Championship Carving Competition in Ocean City, Maryland. It was the first year for World Class entries in interpretive sculpture, and Martin did an elaborate carving of an egret, a common wading bird in central Florida. The bird won the $6,000 first-place award in World Class, and Martin was launched on a full-time carving career.

Since that Cinderella-like beginning, Martin has won many major prizes and has been invited to show his work in the most prestigious exhibitions in the country. In addition to his Ward Competition wins, Martin has won at the Grand Masters Competition and at the Gulf-South in New Orleans, and has been in such heralded juried exhibitions as the Birds in Art show at the Leigh Yawkey Woodson Art Museum in Wausau, Wisconsin, the Southeastern Wildlife Art Exposition in Charleston, the Easton Waterfowl Festival in Maryland, and the fall Ward Foundation exhibition in Salisbury.

Martin is a collector of antique hand tools, and once he roughs out a carving with a bandsaw or chainsaw, he uses a variety of chisels and gouges to refine the work. Martin prefers to carve at the more deliberate pace afforded by hand tools. On most carvings, his use of power tools is limited to the preliminary steps of roughing out.

In this session, Martin carves an eagle head from walnut. The wood is a triple-crotch that was seasoning in Martin's yard for more than two years. Martin wanted to carve an eagle as a tribute to all of those majestic birds, as well as other wildlife, that were lost in the 1989 Alaskan oil spill caused by the grounding of the tanker Exxon Valdez. He decided to carve the eagle in a calling position because he felt it represented the anguish the oil spill exacted on humans and wildlife alike.

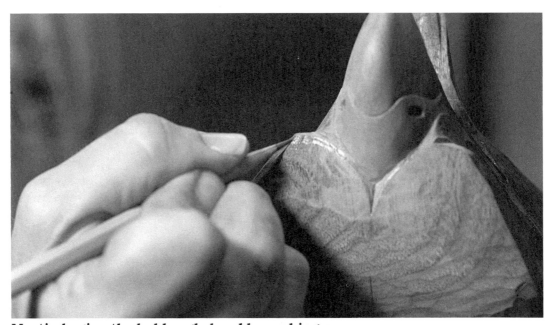

Martin begins the bald eagle head by making a paper pattern of the work, to which he will refer to often ensure that the scale and proportion remain correct. He roughs out the sculpture with a chain saw, then brings it into the studio for refinement. The beak has been completed (see Bird Carving Basics volume 4, *Bills and Beaks*), and Martin has roughed out the head with gouges and knives. He is now ready to begin carving. He starts by sketching the brow area, using photos of eagles as reference.

Next he marks the preliminary location of the eye, again using photographs as reference. This mark will be removed when Martin carves the brow area, but it provides an important benchmark when beginning the carving.

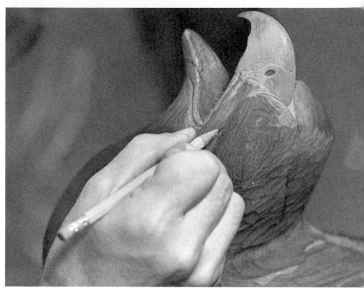

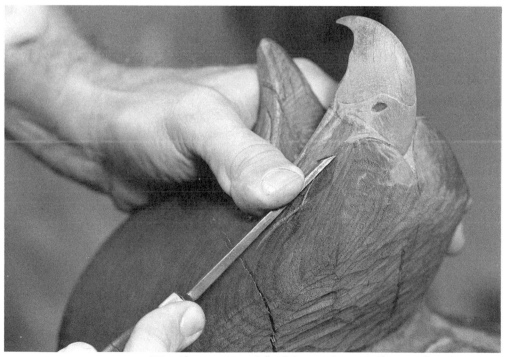

Martin uses a chisel to undercut the eyebrow area. The eagle has a dominant brow, which gives it a noble, somewhat sinister look. Leave plenty of wood when roughing out the carving, Martin advises. "If you don't have enough wood to make the brow dominant, the bird will end up looking like a parrot."

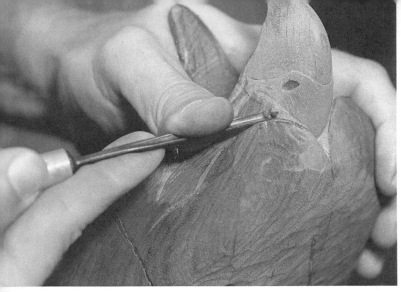

Martin begins carving with a variety of knives, chisels, and gouges, many of which are antiques he purchased in Europe. This gouge is handy for cutting the groove that extends below the brow of the eagle.

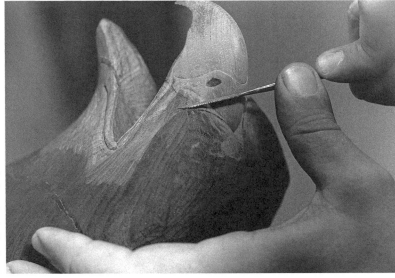

When the groove is established under the brow, Martin uses a riffler, or small rasp, to round off the edges of the brow.

The riffler not only rounds off the brow, it removes the cut marks left by the small gouges.

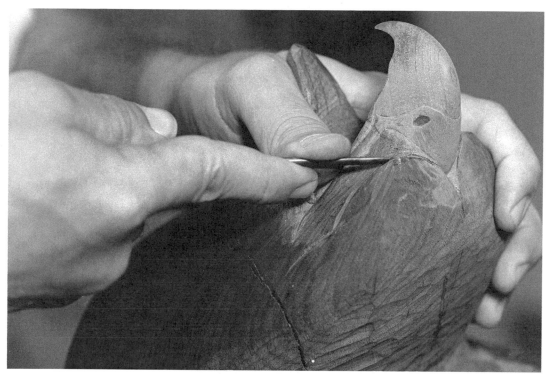

The small chisel is used to remove more wood beneath the brow, just forward of where the eye will be located. Martin frequently moves from the brow to the face of the bird, checking constantly to maintain symmetry.

The cheek area of the eagle is slimmed down with this larger bent gouge. At this stage in the carving Martin is concentrating on the transition between the bill, which has been finished, and the head.

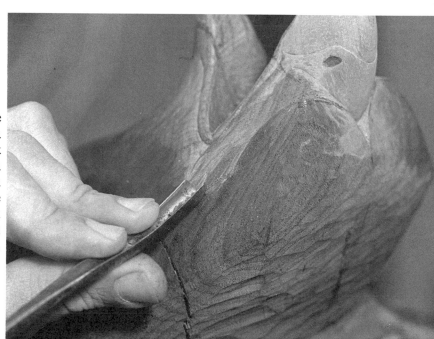

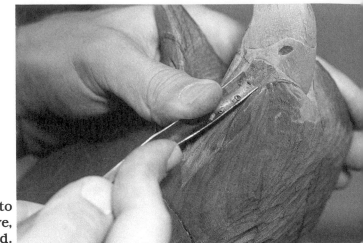

The same tool is used to
smooth the area in front of the eye,
where the bill meets the head.

At this stage, the brow
line has been estab-
lished, and the cheek
has been carved to pro-
vide a smooth tran-
sition with the beak.

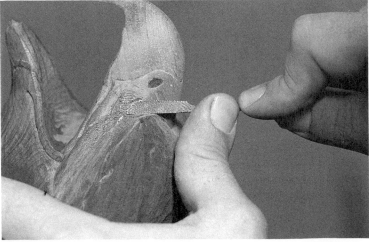

The small riffler is
used to remove tool
marks along the front
of the brow.

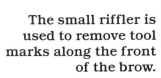

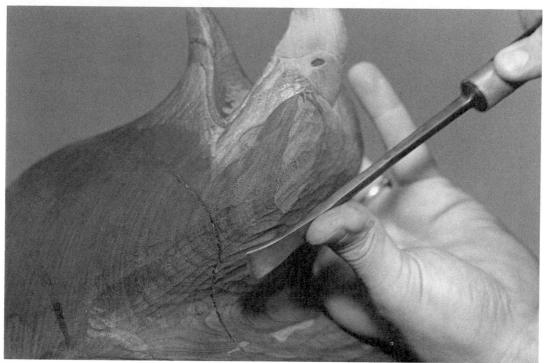

Martin is now ready to begin shaping the back of the head. He won't remove much wood, but enough to make sure that work on the face area doesn't progress too far beyond work on the rest of the head. Martin likes to work over a large area, keeping all steps of the carving process near the same level of completion.

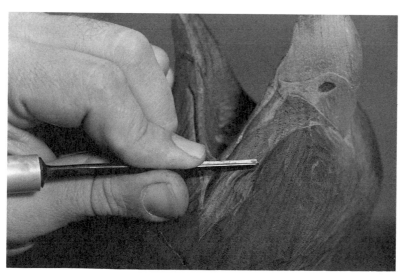

Martin goes back to the eye area, removing a small amount of wood with the small gouge. "You just have to keep undercutting until you get the proper depth," he says.

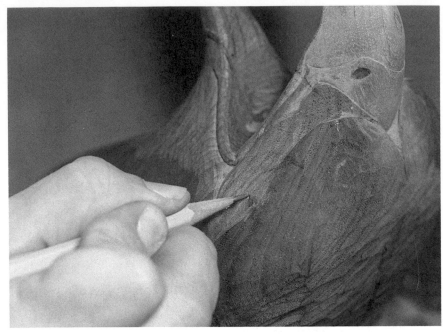

Again he marks the eye location with a pencil. Although he frequently removes the pencil mark when carving, he must redraw it because the eye position dictates the location of other facial features.

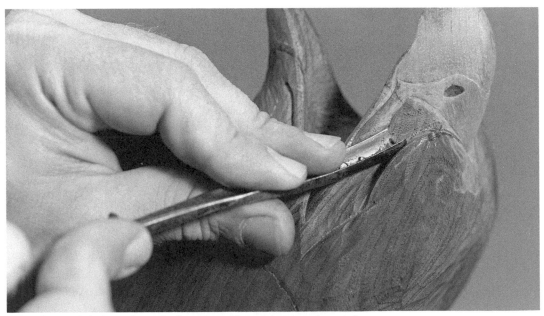

Carving with hand tools is a continuous process of removing wood; Martin again goes back to the eye-line with a larger gouge. "When you get one spot done it affects another spot, so you go around and around until you get it all right," he says. The paper patterns are important benchmarks because they help maintain the proper size and proportion.

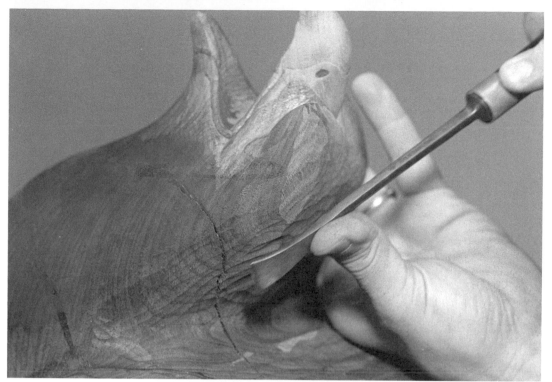

Because this bird is being depicted with its head thrown back, the feathers will be bunched at the back of the neck. Martin leaves a great deal of thickness in this area. The checks and cracks visible in this photo will later be filled with strips of walnut when the sculpture is finished.

This large gouge is good for removing shallow but wide swaths of wood along broad areas such as the back of the eagle's head. Note in this photo how the shape of the brow area on the left side of the head has changed as the carving process has progressed.

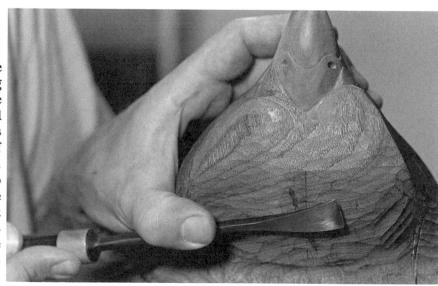

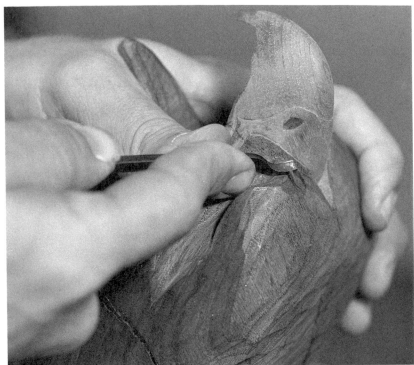

At this point, Martin is preparing to carve the eyes. He uses the small bent gouge to carve the area in front of the eye where the face of the bird joins the cere.

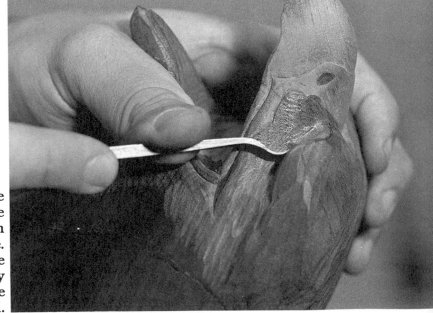

He further defines the brow area where the eye will be located with the small bent gouge. The brow will have to be recessed slightly where the eye will be located.

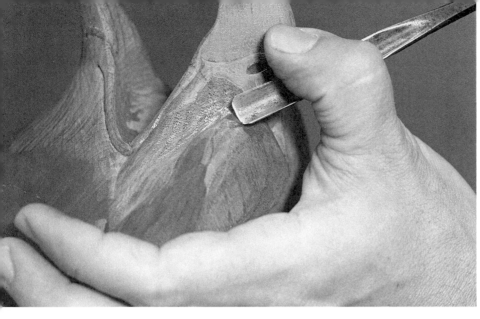

A final
pass with
the larger gouge
smooths the
brow and
readies it for
the eye.

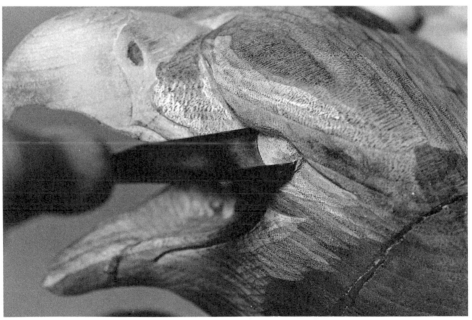

Martin uses a U-shaped gouge to begin the eye.
Once the eye location is marked with pencil, the
gouge is pressed into the wood beneath the brow.
In later steps, the face will be carved to relieve the
eye. It will take several cuts with this gouge, fol-
lowed by knife work on the face, before the eye
takes on the proper relief. Note the slight upward
flare in the brow that accommodates the eye.

Once the eye is established, the area around it will be reduced, making the eye prominent. The line that passes through the eye extends from the front of the head, just under the brow, along the side of the head.

After the eye is cut with the large gouge, Martin uses the small gouges to backcut toward the eyeball, giving it shape and relief.

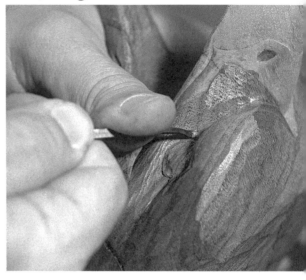

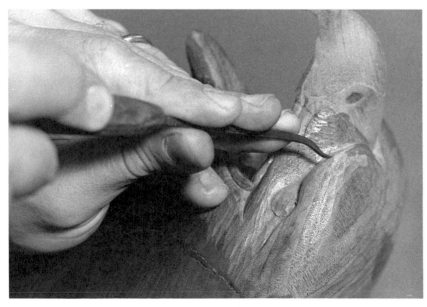

Martin uses the small bent gouge to extend this line toward the front of the head.

It is important that this line run smoothly along the side of the head, creating a proper transition from the beak to the brow to the eye. Martin makes extensive use of reference photographs to determine eye placement in relationship to the brow and the corner of the beak.

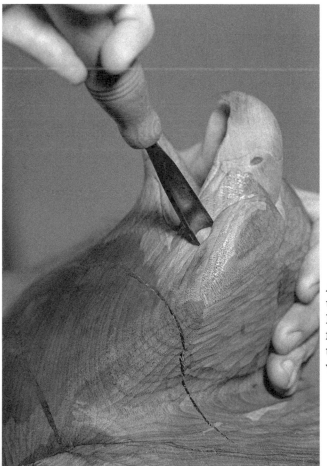

Again the large gouge is used to further define the eye. By backcutting along the face to the eye Martin makes the eye more prominent with each cut.

71

The eye is now more pronounced and is ready to
be carved. The eye must be sufficiently raised
from the face because in subsequent steps Martin
will carve the edges of it, making it appear convex.

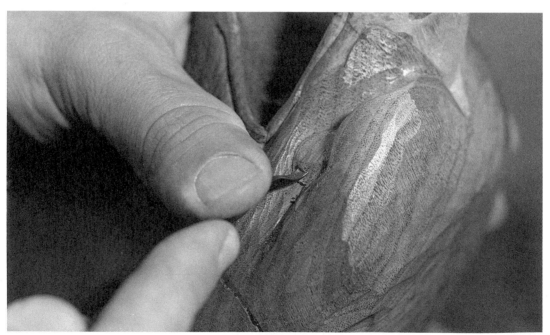

The small bent gouge is used to carefully round
the eyeball.

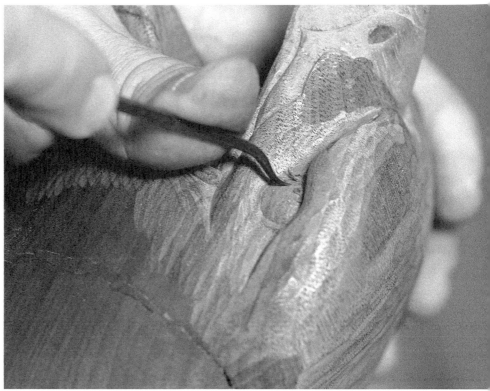

The center part
of the eyeball
is left high, but
it is curved
slightly on the
circumference.

Martin again backcuts toward the eye, removing
wood along the face area to make the eyeball
appear higher and more pronounced.

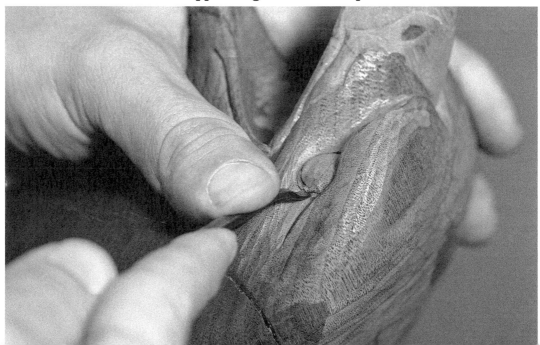

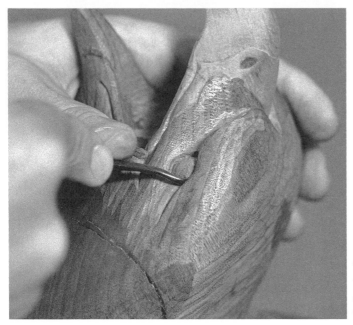

The gouge is used under the brow to help make the eye appear recessed into the brow.

Martin takes a break when his dad, Tom Gates, stops by the studio to check on the eagle's progress. The walnut workpiece is massive; it is actually a triple-crotch turned upside down. It seasoned for several years in Martin's yard before he began the carving, but still it checked slightly when he brought it inside. Most tight-grained woods like walnut will crack and check when brought inside unless they are seasoned extensively beforehand. A rule of thumb for seasoning is one year for each inch of thickness, Martin says.

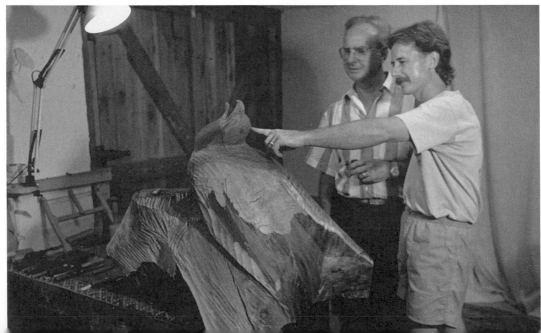

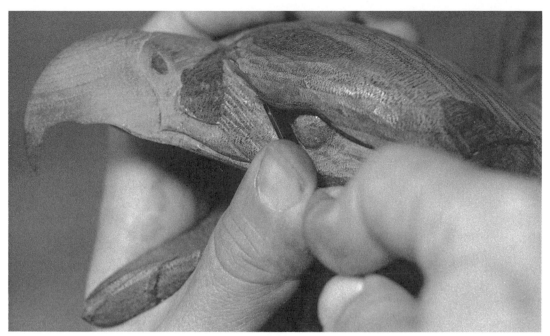

The brow of the eagle must be pronounced. The eye and the brow give the bird personality, and because this bird will not be highly detailed and painted, the few lines the artist uses must convey the desired mood and emotion.

Martin again undercuts the eye, then uses the small gouge to carefully create a convex surface.

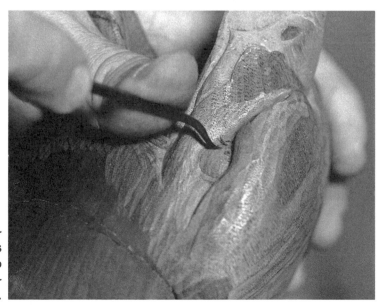

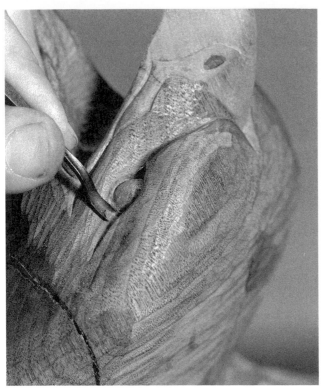

As the groove gains depth and definition, the eagle begins to take on a personality, a "look."

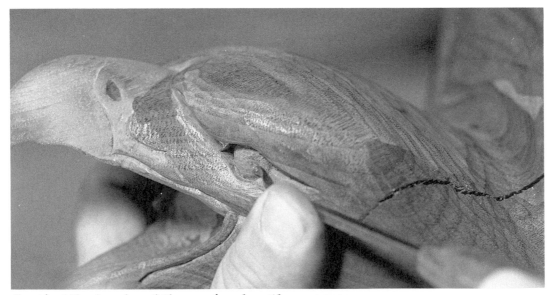

Carving the head and the eye is a lengthy process of "going around and around." Here Martin again uses the gouge to deepen the groove running through the eye position.

Although this will be an interpretive bird with little detail, Martin must still ensure that all lines and gestures are correct to provide the feeling of realism. In the bench behind him are several photographic books of eagles, to which he often refers.

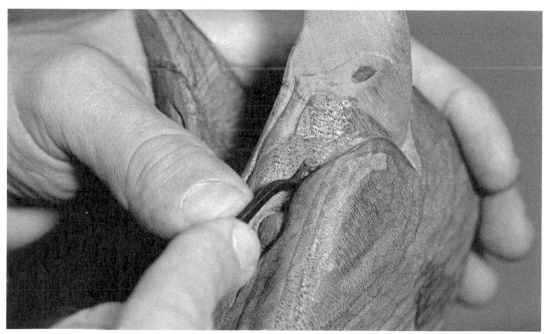

With the eye near completion, the gouge is used to refine the transition between the eye area and the beak area.

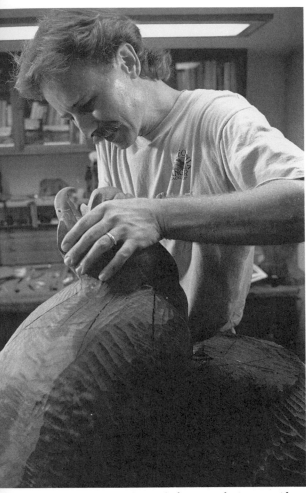

At this stage, Martin knows what he wants to express with the sculpture and has roughed out the position of the wings and tail. He has made paper patterns to keep him on course in the carving process.

When doing an interpretive piece like this large eagle, Martin always begins with the head and lets the body of the bird follow. With somewhat rough wood like this walnut crotch, the wood often dictates the shape and subject of the carving.

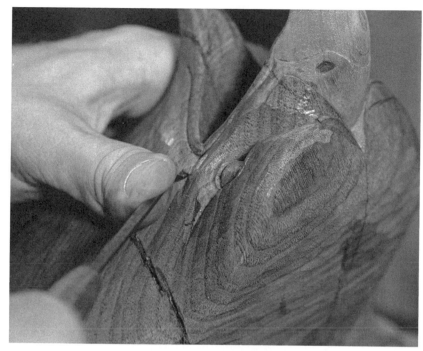

As the head nears completion, he concentrates on refinements, here adding a crease behind the open beak.

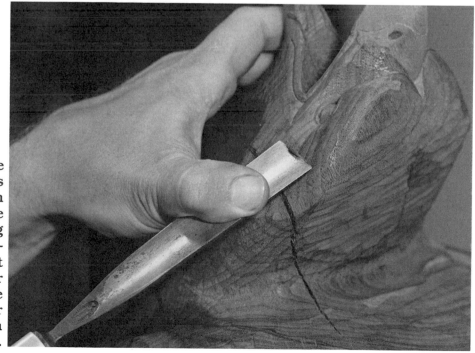

The wide spoon gouge is used to smooth the surface of the carving and to remove marks left by smaller gouges. The checks will later be filled with walnut strips.

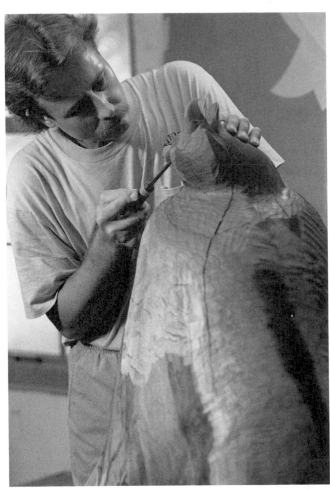

A rear view shows Martin's progress so far.

The expression of the bird can be changed greatly with detail around the eyes and mouth. Martin decides to further deepen the eye groove to create more emotion in the carving.

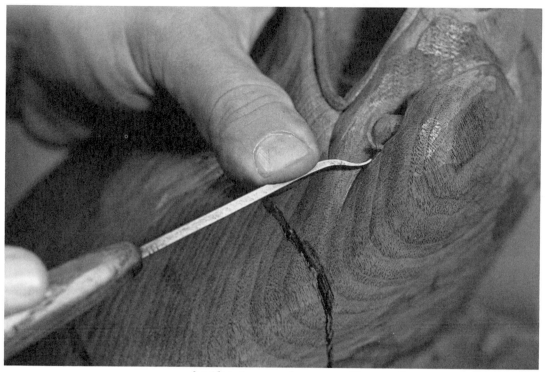

As the groove deepens, the eye becomes more pronounced; Martin backcuts toward the eye to give it more relief.

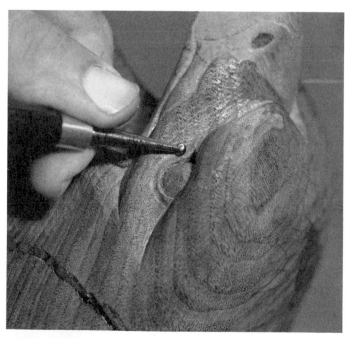

As a final step, he uses the steel burnishing tool to compress the wood fibers and give the wood lustre. Later, he will apply numerous coats of Watco oil finish.

With the carving completed, though the wood is still unfinished, the head appears lifelike.

Several weeks after the photo session, Martin became dissatisfied with the lines around the beak of the eagle, so he changed them slightly to give the bird a more anguished expression. Note in this photo that the line behind the beak curves downward, changing the expression of the bird. Numerous coats of hand-rubbed oil finish give the walnut a rich, deep patina. The eagle was exhibited for the first time at the 1989 Ward Wildfowl Art Exhibition in Salisbury, Maryland.

About the Author

Curtis Badger has written widely about wildfowl art, wildfowl hunting, and conservation issues in general. His articles have appeared in many national and regional magazines, and he serves as editor of *Wildfowl Art Journal,* which is published by the Ward Foundation. He is currently working with carver Jim Sprankle on a book on wildfowl painting techniques, and he is writing a book about growing up on the Virginia coast. He lives in Onley, Virginia.

Other Books of Interest to Bird Carvers

Songbird Carving with Ernest Muehlmatt
Muehlmatt shares his expertise on painting, washes, feather flicking, and burning, plus insights on composition, design, proportion, and balance.

Waterfowl Carving with J. D. Sprankle
A fully illustrated reference to carving and painting twenty-five decorative ducks.

Carving Miniature Wildfowl with Robert Guge
Scale drawings, step-by-step photographs, and painting keys demonstrate the techniques that make Guge's miniatures the best in the world.

Decorative Decoy Designs
Bruce Burk's two volumes (*Dabbling and Whistling Ducks* and *Diving Ducks*) are complete guides to decoy painting by a renowned master of the art. Both feature life-size color patterns, reference photographs, alternate position patterns, and detailed paint-mixing instructions for male and female of twelve duck species.

Bird Carving Basics: Eyes
Volume one in the series presents a variety of techniques on how to insert glass eyes, carve and paint wooden eyes, burn, carve with and without fillers, and suggest detail. Featured carvers include Jim Sprankle, Lee Osborne, Pete Peterson, and Grayson Chesser.

Bird Carving Basics: Feet
Volume two features the same spectacular photography and detailed step-by-step format. Techniques for making feet out of wood, metal, and epoxy, creating texture and tone, and shaping feet in various positions are demonstrated by Dan Brown, Jo Craemer, and Larry Tawes, Jr.

Bird Carving Basics: Bills and Beaks
Volume four illustrates different ways to create wildfowl bills, such as burning and wrinkling, inserting a bill, using epoxy membranes, making open and closed bills, and carving the tongue. Experts like Jim Sprankle, Mark McNair, and Martin Gates share their innovative techniques.

For ordering information and a complete list of carving titles, write:
Stackpole Books
P.O. Box 1831
Harrisburg, PA 17105
or call 1-800-READ-NOW